I0554729

PARENTAL FOREST

POEMS BY
CHAD NORMAN

What first comes to mind is his focus on Mother Earth and all the life She gives and sustains; Chad writes about humanity in its everyday essence, the good, the bad, and the ugly. Poetry about birds, animals, trees, and the connection with human beings, each with their own characteristic behaviours pour out in beautifully crafted words and arranged in masterful fluidity.

- Stephen Agustine, Executive Director, Donald Marshall Junior Institue, Cape Breton University

Chad Norman has created a wonderful book of poetry full of joy and wonder, self reflection, optimism and love. He has always delivered amazing collections of words connected together to make beautiful sentences. With these he is able to share what is in his heart, and help make the world in his head come alive in your heart.

- Julie Pellisher-Lush, poet

Chad Norman's new collection is full of unexpected gratitude: to crows and robins, to a chipmunk and "the joyful chickadees," to a crocus emerging from snow during the first weeks of a pandemic. In these heartfelt poems, nature offers both solace and challenge. Norman shows us that, clinging "to whatever will allow us / to come out together," we can draw comfort from human solidarity as from the fragile, imperilled natural world.

- Mark Abley, poet

Chad Norman's book of poetry reminds me of a butterfly flying through my memory. On its journey, it lands on something of interest that will stimulate your imagination. It is truly magical collection."

- Alan Syliboy, Mi'kmaw Artist

AOS PUBLISHING, 2024
AOS POETRY, 2024

ISBN: 978-1-990496-20-2

Cover Design: Jessica James

Visit AOS Publishing's website:
www.aospublishing.com

for Val and Barb,
sisters who live lives open to the
mysteries of the Wild.

ACKNOWLEDGEMENTS

Some of these poems have appeared previously in:

Metafora, (Polish Anthology, 2020), Boston Literary Magazine, Nova Scotia Advocate, Pendemic, Impspired, (England), Strands Litsphere, Voices Israel Anthology (2020), Poetry Pacific, Event Magazine, Queen's Quarterly, Time Of The Poet Anthology (Canada/Africa), Spotlight 28, Gathering In, (Nova Scotia Covid-19 Anthology, 2020), Revista Azahar, Poetry Pause, Blank Spaces Magazine, Live Encounters, 11th Anniversary Edition, Grihaswamini International e-magazine, International Human Rights Art Festival, Black Dog & One-Eyed Press, (Masked Anthology, 2022), Under The Azure Anthology(2021), Fromicaleone (Italy), Mock-Up Magazine (Italy), WordCity Monthly, Pocket Lint, The Poetry Kit, Banchetful (Romania), Urmuz Magazine (Romania), Lothlorien Poetry Journal, Kamesta Magazine (Peru), The Poet, Eufeme (Portugal), Setu, World Poetry Tree (Dubai), Athanor (Romania), Vita Brevis Press (USA), Van Choung (Vietnam), Polis Magazine (Greece), Write-Up International Anthology (India), Ibbetson St. Magazine (USA), Articoli Liberi (France).

And I wish to thank Ruth who owns, guards, and pays the taxes on the property where the small parental forest exists; she has no idea the immense importance my unwanted treks, over nearly 15 years, have become in order to keep sane enough to capture the poems I was given each time I chose and dared to walk through it.

I also wish to thank Michael and Lainee, for their on-going love and support. And the staff at AOS, for the decision to bring this book to the world. May you, the reader, now feel and enjoy the gifts I hope these poems offer.

Table of Contents

WHAT A WINDOW EXTENDS THE EYE

To look
at a tree
and wonder
how many leaves
can catch
a drop of rain,
or support
a wasp wandering
in the shade.

TRYING TO UNDERSTAND ANOTHER ELECTION

They say, "She is a cat."
They say, "She is not a sparrow."

Out there on the front deck
the tailless sparrow seeks the seed
and Simona simply watches,

but deep in her brain
her teeth seem excited
more than I can know.

Why I am the home-owner here
has nothing to do with
sparrow in her well-fed feline mind,
chirps spoken each day –
it being the only loud one,
the one listened to, at least.

They say, "I am a voter."
They say, " I must vote."
They say, or we can say,
sparrow, Simona, and myself,
no one will take us away
from our political conquests.

Now, look closer,
yes, all three of us,
do seem to be smiling.

TO BE TAUGHT

Alone with the virus
as May actually made it
when I walk and watch
how the robins hear
worm after worm.
I enjoy, then revere
such steady harmony,
activated knowledge
of being, alive and
absolutely unnecessary.

TIM'S CUP

Sometimes a walk within the ripening Wild
other years when it was May
opened both the active eyes
of the man I still become
to what I am willing to bet much on –
two different scenes connected by a dream –
he, Tim Horton, far from the icy blue-lines
seated at the unset kitchen table
staring into a cup of coffee
as his gleaming spoon went round and round
seeing at least the first of the franchises.

As for the other scene my money is on
one unseen in his steaming brew
as the famous morning poured into his eyes
fortunately unable to witness unlike mine
his legendary name on each cup
thrown from a truck, carried on a car-roof,
dropped by a drunk, left to be litter
either in the grass by the forest, or
in the forest ending the fern, or
right there under foot every ten feet.

Regardless, I doubt the great player
would want to be turning over
in the grave where his career rests
with the knowledge fans were that forgetful.

THE WEIGHT OF A STRANGER

When a woman
who has been
treated poorly
by another man
chooses to turn
your help
into a session of
flirtation, even
though you offered
a journey to
the distance, the one
you learned from
when a boy,
how she gave it
the track of her life,
being married
for all those years
but still came out
for who knows why,
to check out your invitation,
your new male energy.
You doubt it
now that she can
accuse you of it,
flirtation, even the
sway into the sexual
where she already
ran her problems
fastly, sadly, aground.

What was wrong
was hers, wasn't part
of any song, a song
you once heard
at Christmas
when you were looking for
nothing to do with

the ear, just a candle
to light
and see fire be
what it has always been.

THE TRUST OF A ROBIN ON SUNDAY
For Gord Downie

No other day than that day
I fed the crows beneath the flags,
one for Nova Scotia, and
one for our country, Canada,
the lone bird three parking spaces
down the paved, well-traipsed hill,
sat in the shadows of trees known
because of the seasons' kind teachings.

And did not move, or fly away
all the time I was there, even
when I stood still and stared at it,
a robin, and it knew in that stare
something I may never know about,
our similar obvious lack of hurry.

Perhaps the bird
simply brilliant enough
to trust its decisions
to not allow me
any superiority over the choice,
its choice, to enjoy the day of rest,
soon to endure the return
to a more southern shade.

Casa Harris, Truro, NS,
August 28, 2016

THE SUN BRINGS US OUT

I touch
the tops of
the tiny fir trees
after what
I thought would be
the last of our
late winter snowfalls,
and it is
in that rare moment,
kind of like
watching a man
whose skin is not
the colour of mine
walking by
carrying
a baby palm tree,
I marvel
and chuckle at
what the
human hands can do.

THE STORY OF A NEW MAN

What the music makes me
want to do
wouldn't, couldn't, & shouldn't
be defined as violence,
after all look at what
has happened to rock n' roll
if you dare, if you care, if you
remember how to share;

I am sure the stillness
of a home
when I'm not there
becomes a loud silence,
no longer a contributor
to what any plastic products
always demand from
a family man caught up
in the raising of a boy
who will never work there;

knowing the filth now
in the lungs of
some aging stepfathers,
who may be poets
lost in the longing of
so many other poets
past or present or so ready
to take up the violence
the music shakes out
more than once when
the home's silence is insistent;

even though the world waits
behind so many of the
innocent basement's faulty windows.

THE SPEECHLESS PUDDLE

I am alone. But with my self.

Prayers have taken me
I want to say nowhere.

But there is the word, "But",
I seek an answer from instead,
mired, no, comfortable in
a depth where anger feels
good, feels exactly where I
should be, no matter how lonely
the body and mind I trust feels.

At the moment I ask
and ask and ask isn't hardship,
a stop I don't need to make at sixty one.

I imagine the clouds in you
passing in the brown water
unable to reflect the sky's blue.

I wanted some help
for my age and my body
but I was a fool again, I was
forgetting how each time
I felt free of the filthy lucre's
ability to stifle the mirror.

Stop me from hearing what
my reflection has always said,
better than anything I hoped for
after any prayer.

Me, standing there
in front of
that piece of strange glass

told I must once again enter
the possibilities in making windows
may somehow bring to alleviate,
start up another phase of control
only meant to pay off a few bills.

The speechless puddle out with me
on a walk I wish would take me
out of this life, lead me like a guide
to a river where I can board
a boat shaped like the word, "Why?"

I am alone still... happily alone.

THE SOLOIST

Often on certain sunny
late fall afternoons
an ailing aging man who
seems to enjoy weekly walks
is brought to a
point of total stoppage
under the shimmer of
sun through leaping leaves,
a brief moment of
 immaculate hearing
as he watches how
 his lengthy shadow
causes the lone cricket's
nearby solo to grow cautious,
until he steps back onto
 the path he has made,
the lowering brightness
 almost like a conductor
waving that wand to
ask the solo to resume,
rising out of a bush
 able to turn from green
to a loud pleasant red.

THE NOISEAHOLICS

Listening to the endless racket
of old men in love with
their leaf-blowers and lawnmowers

to throw a rake
in their mindless piles
destined for the plastic bags
they set at the curb in order
to magically vanish;

the idea of them making noise
obviously escapes any mental capacity
they should have,

the simple thought, perhaps,
missed out on
due to their hearing aids
all being turned off
or requiring new batteries.

THE MOTHER OF NATURE

The curves of her breasts
come into the picture,

the man in me
who is to be taught
understands little
about such a scene.

I manage the ice
she hides under the snow,
aware of possible injury
as the icicles
appear as nipples
for familiar crows to suckle,

all of them a lesson
I actually learn from,
each sipping beak
an invitation into reverence.

Could this be
the mother of nature?

I hope so,
she is the only one
able to remove any
inability to see,
to really see
her incontestable beauty
without a fool's arousal.

THE LITTLE PINE

To rest on a fallen tree
in front of
the little pine,

all the time crows
avoid the gulls' theft,
find all my hand served.

I feel loneliness being helped,
dead needles are left,

a courage, to go on,
has returned,

as a circle
of melting ice
surrounds
the chubby trunk.

THE JOURNEY MAN
For Norm

There is a man I can honour
perhaps lying in a bed with the mind
life has helped him to now explore,
the mind he turned to throughout his living
each day and was not left without answers,
was not left without the courage to question.
His present exploration allows little travel,
halls full of doorways, his wheelchair heading
to what some of us know to be the last door,
know deep within us is to be the best door,
one he knows too will take him from that bed,
take and stand him on the shore of the pearly lake
shining and unfished in that elsewhere now ready.
Life has helped him, and the prairie upbringing too,
stories he may not recall sharing are recalled
without much hesitation, how as a boy and young teen
it was the potatoes meal after meal there to feed
his brothers, his sisters, the father, and the mother,
so many meals of potatoes, so many other stories
he didn't share being the eldest son, being the one
getting away from the endless view, the beautiful
flatness.

Out of the two parents it was mother who held on,
she with all those years behind her had expectations
for the simple, for what all mothers when seated alone
expect, the visit, the one son she always called first,
the one son who due to his appearance changed her,
introduced a union made of pain and joy and
womanhood.
The visit, he too knew what it meant, leaving the trade
he sought, the studies, the move to coast and city,
 to be with her at so many ages, even her less hearty
years.
On that West Coast the classes and friend-filled nights
held him in a kind necessary embrace,

16

perhaps a journey was anxious to unfold,
anxious to offer him to more than one path,
the exceptional fork, a direction
few see early in their pursuit of themselves,
in pursuit of a certainty, one he would enjoy
but never include in the stories,
 a certainty that comes about after education pays off,
the pursued trade part of the history of Christ's history.
Other provinces beckoned to him, there was work and
money,
how he could see his country,
how he could grow himself not only through his trade,
but through being led again away from the Pacific,
in to the interior where orchards and campgrounds could
become a home,
a new living, a community of heat, mountains,
the point thrown out in a lake where footprints in
summer
could be left behind the stroll in the blacktop,
a community a mile or so off the border inhabited
by so many fine Portuguese wine makers.
A place where one marriage would give the gift of
children,
would eventually end after a job, to build a sunroom
and not notice the unhappy blonde woman
long past what the sun was supposed to heal,
her marriage ready to leave in the dark.
The walks started, he and her, campground and
sunroom,
both meeting out in what both wanted, a chance to
escape the mutual,
the lack of, the unbearable routine, the homes no longer
able to comfort,
the families no longer able to lie,
a chance to extend more of their journeys,
their need to seek another possibility to love, to leave the
mountains,
to merge into the daring, to be a couple,
to settle both of their losses and establish a roof of their
own,

a love-affair meant to flourish.
Down in where the Stetson and stampede are known
he opened a shop where wood became CEO's desks,
where wood was asked to become counters for banks,
where he saw goals become a company, where the
gold star took its place as logo, where Swiss craftsmen
were hired, were given jobs far from their homeland,
were to become one man who had married his sister,
the sister with a smile no cancer could snuff out,
one man, brother-in-law, part of all the quality products,
part of what both knew, how wood should be leaving
their shop.

Life in Cowtown was set up in the southeast side, where
the driveway once held a number of Dodge Challengers,
one white and pink, one an irresistible orange and black,
and the convertible with a 440 under the hood, ready to
be driven as a test,
as proof, as the most memorable drive a young man
would remember,
due to speeds down a hill causing such an unknown fear,
a rush no drug could circulate.
He opened this world to the children, his and Carole's, a
world they paid into,
they knew as a bed and meals, they entered this new
family,
curious, definitely part of, each very individual.
When the Boom went quiet, he heard the loudness of
change
within what that city had made him, no cowboy,
no white-collared oil-soaked cliché – he heard what
change was saying,
where change was pointing,
and with the children from both sides gone in their
directions,
the loudness grew to a volume
he heard as a voice, an old voice, saying the old journey is
on,
the old journey he had heard so many times, once more
new and as before,

familiar to the point of packing, sifting through
what was so important it had to be kept,
had to be him in some way.
There may have been a moment when he sought to see
somehow between the identical houses across the street
even the tips,
the tops, of the Rockies, even a glimpse of snow he would
never witness melting,
disappearing, always the view to cause the longing,
to be the direction he sought, the decision once more
meaning a move was vital, a move meant to provide
this the next journey a chance to locate a valley of
opportunities,
a valley where he built windows, gave back some of the
views.
A new home, known outside of his windows as Vedder,
located yes, in the valley, the Fraser Valley, just barely
outside of Chilliwack,
under, in the distance, Mount Cheam, where he gave
back, not only views,
but to himself, a house with a pool those he loved would
enjoy,
would find themselves in, being away from their financial
bouts
and allowed to relocate family, floating in the heated
water
he was in charge of, Pool Owner, Father, Grandfather,
there was no need
to add "step" to any thing, his love given in ways all sides
knew as the real,
the love each had coming, the love seldom spoke of, his
way of including,
his way of making the families one.
To follow him was some of the son's and daughter's and
their babies' way,
he again left another residence to find a cozy place above
a lake,
a place the valley sent him to, a place where three new
valleys met
above a lake, where eagles taught young to hunt ducks,

where trains on the shoreline of the other side were too long to watch disappear,
where weathers came up all three valleys throughout the days,
where there was a peak further up, known as Bastion Mountain,
always a drive he would set as a challenge,
but family had to be ready to go up with him,
an experience he offered during the stay
they had phoned to plan, always getting away from some crazed city.

Bastion. Something considered a stronghold.
May those he took up understand now his reasons of insistence,
may his smiles during the drive provide the answers
about why he wanted to reach that peak
with others he loved, smiles he kept for so many gifts he gave,
smiles he hopes someone noticed, he had when on the height,
he had when in someone else's low spot,
smiles even now lying in a bed, or taking a
walk however, or wherever he wishes, happily out of the halls of another bastion,
a bastion of care, ending up at his last earned door,
ending his journeys, those he shared, those where
hard work and laughter were the two he gave,
working side-by-side, or if miles were between us.

Casa Harris
September 26, 2013
Truro, NS

THE ID COVE 20
For Ruth K.

I sneak outside
during the virus invasion
to privately witness
vigilance comes
in the form of
a wee purple crocus
poking out of
our morning's snowfall.

THE BROKEN NEWS
*In memory of those Colchester County
lost April 18-19, 2020*

It,
all for a few moments
seems so far away,
in another community,
another province,
another country.

And then in another few moments
it is right there
in our stomachs,
our hearts,
and then down our cheeks.

It,
deserved of such a description
I will not say otherwise
other than
it has paused the tides.

THE BIRTH OF SHADE

1.
Limitations. Limited. Limits.
Why acknowledge the unfriendly
especially when a fellow man
who came across otherwise
having once returned my hello?

Actually there is no question there,
I mean why should he come out
from the safety of changing trees,
chosen by friendly feathered ones
to protect new invisible nests.

2.
Thank you, chipmunk.
Your astounding tail in the breeze
what manages to find us in here
where a fly lands on a hand.

I keep my fingers full of
one peanut at a time, you
from the Wild also give a gift
I try to tell means so much
to the man I sit inside of now.

Your tail again, again, & again
sunlit in the wind educates
about how I know so little,
you choose to feast on the peanut
taken, teaching me more about trust.

THE BEAUTY OF A THISTLE

As the days of the week charge off somewhere
the early morning jaunts to the job
provide a mind pondering what it is
to know a blessing, to be blessed, to want
blessedness, almost thought after thought.

As each step up the hill changes the thoughts
to a curious surge throughout the body,
perhaps a feeling coming on as the sun
rises higher behind me, to allow the shade
to remain just that, and the warming light
to find and rest upon the purple of blooms.

New growth as summer ages, as the choice
now seems a wise one, the lawn needed cut,
I chose to do the backyard first, being higher,
and as the blades, one by one, were lowered
the choice to go around the young thistle
now understood, now being a site of beauty,
now being walked past, as a smile takes over
my face, and the dew dampens my old boots.

Casa Harris,
Truro, NS
July 22, 2016

THE BACKYARD BIRTH

I see the neighbourhood tree
has finally given birth
to a swaying baby swing.

The brand new lengths of rope
two bright yellow umbilical cords
tied tightly to the heights
of a sturdy leafless mother.

Every second day I walk by them
on what was an empty avenue
a witness to this quiet delivery
tolerating the dog-walker take-over
due to discoveries of full little bags
left beside the power-poles and curbs
or thrown under flowering shrubs.

Today is different, the swing is grown,
has become a mother too
but the child is not there,
no one pushes, a barren place
I, in my imagination, see pregnant
one day when the virus unlocks
the backyard, laughter for the future.

SURVIVAL: HERE I AM!
For Nicoleta

My foot in a favourite slipper
taps just above the carpet
installed years ago,
across the room filled
with the songs of Bad Co.
making me cry,
feel for the days I was fifteen.

Here I am back with Mystery
or am I moving ahead
holding its hand not knowing
a thing about the future,
standing nonetheless on "Only",
a place I was afraid of,
standing though, only, only, only...

Steps continue to be effective
one, still after, one, how to
be about survival, how
I will survive again, moving
still, an older man I want,
an older thought of who he is,
or, perhaps, an older me now ready
for the newness I know nothing about.

I see the bird feeder is being soiled.
I revere the birds unafraid of the storm.

Here I am,
asking for nothing,
with no hands brought to a prayer,
here I am
setting out to help the crows
who always have an answer first.

SPRING IS NOT JUST ANOTHER SEASON

1. The Nest Builders

Planting,
can a nest be like a seed?

Under a kitchen window
in the unclipped cedars
a man notices the building
of her choice, a robin I
come to know is a female.

A choice that happened before
eight years ago to be exact
in practically the same tree
just a few branches over –
she, maybe the same one
or another flown in
to be the courageous mother.

It may not be the time
to say she knows more
than what a gaze teaches
or how a sight from the past
ends up being so important,
wings continue to fortify the build.

In those cedars only branches give
the brief red-breasted gifts,
first him and then her
mated without question.

This is where we meet
a distant trusting chipmunk,
another not part of humanity
on top of the lonely boulder,
there's a longing to tell of

all the choices other than
what is under skin, with fur,
with the wings ready to be
how food will reach furious beaks.

Waiting becomes a necessary education.
When will the chipmunk arrive,
now I know they can choose to kill.
Perhaps my bellow needs to be scarier.

All that is voices somewhere far off,
a racket not to accompany her
riveted skills in building what
must be a vision, after all
we build homes for our young
without any fear we have no wings
or an ability to construct in branches.

2. The Egg Bearers

A choice overwhelms days chosen
due to clarity, yes, even a sanity
to be easily led by all the birds
choosing the yard I tend reluctantly,
one now taking on an importance
longing to bring more life into it.

The wondrous "it" a red breast scans
no matter what the male may try,
she chooses where the eggs will be laid.
I notice how her colour improves bushes,
out there in the street though being
problematic for the stupid and arrogant,
colour, how skin is such a spokesperson
but feathers replace both, how yearning
becomes longing for unity in branches
of a tree or what humanity hopes to become.

She discards anything a man would call crazy,

his mind unable to be in a bird's brain
having never had the ability of a beak
to take up the mud and grass
a nest the eggs will warm and hatch in,
hatching I hope eyes in my head
will allow needs in my mind
to believe some kind of protection
is possible by sneaking daily peeks
out of the kitchen window; she & he
notice only what the building becomes
until darkness in the nest is no longer dark,
where she has left three dim blue lights,
oval in shape, not there to see
or know, to be with what doesn't survive.

3. The Hatchling Feeders

What is it? Something about
how tears fall into an empty sink,
little beaks waiting, now visible,
as the day finds a way through branches
with a sun from the east the window
seems to take in like a mother of sorts.

Your new beaks such triangles
ready even though a weakness
propels you forward, it isn't always
the mother or father thrusting,
you reach, you want, you are
the new ones, but do they know,
do mother and father possess any
of it I see? All the reasons I stand
on tippy-toes after drying dishes
to be the one able to see new life.

A nest in branches given by a tree
a tree with no knowledge of a nest,
what the robins chose to build there –

think about it, to come back two years
in a row, and someone saw that choice,
what brought about young in the dark
other than when some sun snuck in
when morning was for the both of us.

I can't, won't keep asking to see them,
yes, life can be, or the world asking
for more seeing how I am human,
just one man trying to be devoted
to moving his species beyond devolution.

Oh, yes, know that. He talks sense. One
little man seeking nothing more than
himself, never mind all the distractions
living casts among him, a planet has
grown to be other than a garden,
quite like hopes when his garden grows.

But there above the sink, his sneak-peeks
begin a slogan to take-over a mind open:
" I love to watch robins making decisions",
how she sits on the front of their nest,
how she rests on the back on their nest,
no proof is needed when time comes
to move into it and cover her hungry ones.

4. The Vicious Theft

Four young at the bottom I count
all a challenge in some little way
I being a witness even at this point
trying to show them a human is wise,
is equipped to share, even with a window
between us, trying after each peek
to be one without any thought
attack would be what comes to end us.

Us, male, male, female, before it
happened, another sleep all of us

woke to curse and chose to share
blaming all interruption on the snoring,
an accusation robins couldn't hear
what the waking worms left alone.

Such food reached the babies' bellies
one night they slept without worry,
how I know this is how I watched
her, their mother, settled herself down
around all of them, nothing tonight
said would be what I found later
after in the morning after the doctor.

I ended what was the appointment,
how a man was in need of answers
robins would be birds, be about
none of any need for a doctor,
living with branches, seasons, life
only they know, without kitchens
and windows I used to usher in
differences we shared, skin being
unlike feathers, witness to birth
featuring no shells, only how I
had to find the nest out of
the cedar's branches, left by the
attacker over at the base of
a neighbour's brick planter, left
there by what could be the answer
I sought holding the dried gathering
of mud and grass, where all of what
was to be a family with the red breasts
to come, little songs when the sun
simply shone on the tops of trees,
and whatever stole what they
tried to bring and give once
regardless of anything human.

5. The Mates Move On

I feel it, I feel my mouth

longing, forming, words never
spoken before, I try to say, I lose it,
worms grow louder, I see her loss,
I see her eyes, he, her mate, no longer
able to be located, I can hear them now,
all the grass has nothing any longer to give.

A nest is no more, the foe has been fed,
so I suggest worms, how to hear them,
perhaps like before all this, spring is
not just another season, and such
a removal is our reminder of
this horrific hunger-fed act.

I seem to learn something watching again,
the mates now in a new yard
hearing how worms somehow live
beneath the perfect poisoned lawn,
seeking meals for themselves now.

SOMEHOW

When the yellow leaf
wriggles in the wind
above a dying fir tree
known as Doug the Third,
it becomes
in the quiet of the Memory
a yellow butterfly
seeking the last
of the bean blooms
in a garden put to rest
before the first of the frosts.

SNOW GULLS

After the ability
to steal, gobble down
most of the dog food
given for the crows' hunger,
even gulping whole unshelled peanuts,
I see the next big decision
comes up during a brief flight
and then comes down to
what power-pole to land on,
will provide the best view
if and when the human wishes
to share a few handfuls of reverence
and go against the unwary winter.

SLEEP WITH A GRIN

After the paid-for hydro
has been turned off
is when the masterpieces begin
to hang themselves,
none of them ever painted
or photographed before,
none of them seen or critiqued
by the corrupt microscope,
connected to
that which belittles
the human potential
a scene and exception
grew up with,
was given to take
in hand
and write about,
not like a baton or torch,
or any such useless connection
to useless competition.

We endure, now, don't we?
The planet our feet expects,
always there.

Nothing surprises us anymore;
we know it all.

Every scene of beauty is about the human.
No flaw, unlike the real Nature,
nothing wrong.

Sleep with a grin, why not?
Sleep and laugh,
go there, find a way,
suitable for yourself,
and stop all to grin,
and if you can find a mirror,

find it,
the watching of a grin,
the seeing of a grin,
a grin your face saves for you,
your face endures for itself,
sleep with a grin,
and make sure there is someone
beside you, or ready
to peer down at you ready,
ready in the morning
to guarantee it was there.

After the fire has been lit
and the home is heating,
the home the System said
you were worthy to own
and beauty is now found
in leaves you rake, is found
in a lawn you keep from
being always trimmed,
is found in a frosted mug
full of liquor from afar,
after the day is a bit lighter,

and Winter is ready
to offer Spring,
a go at the seasons
you use to stay sane.

SIPPING A PALE ALE ONE SUMMER
For Jean M.

I almost felt the joy
found when a breeze
is in the grass
under some trees
now finished shading
some kind of trouble
growing inside of the
body I have at sixty,
taken from my eyes
and what they give
to forget I am aging,
I am becoming a man
unable to escape trust
in the mystery of being,
or this brief being alive.

RANDOM STANZAS IN MEMORY OF HEATHER SPEARS (1935-2021)

I wish
to take
your face in the
trusty fingers my hands
have to offer,
all the wish
wants to be.

I sit
on a
stone waiting in a hope
as sturdy as it is
with a second wish,
to see the chipmunk
April-chill brought close
during another
Nova Scotia spring.

I think
of Yevtushenko's I,
how he
stood alone in a country
when 1950's Russia
had the poets we now read,
when we take advantage
of his available words.

I walk
out into the mellow year
even though a virus
rules us
regardless of hair left uncut,
and certain arses
left unkicked

there in the house
occupied by liars
who worship white skin.

I cry
knowing not what to do
with the news
of you and your eighty six years
leaving us,
only to feel the hugs
shared there in Copenhagen,
shared in the sun
finding the windows
of your thankful gallery.

PARENTAL FOREST

I have been touched.
I have been entered.

And now you're in me.
And now you're helping me.

I can only tell you
the moon isn't super, just full.

I see it that way,
but you won't believe me,
will you?

Somewhere along the walk
the cold is very cold,
everything I am in,
dressed, hooded, gloved,
just a shivering man.

Trying can describe
some of it,
this living I do,
I have here in me,
this living being more
than me, being a big view.

Being a view with no size.
Just something to lead
all that is in me
ready for all of a song,
a poem, leading all of this
into ourselves, into,
some place all of us eventually find,
and will stand for,
that deepness we feel
when trust is the teacher,
the path, the hand,

the eye, the voice,
a little spot to claim
without any fanfare.

Just a voice I've trusted,
a voice not a parent,
a voice not an adult,
what I take steps toward
no matter a past
when a boy hated
everything his father ordered,
all the words I used
to become unlike him.

None of all that said
means anything anyway
if I wish to hide from it,
from him, a past, so long ago,
what does mean and always has
finds one spot to survive
each and every lovable season.

In there he is long gone.
In there I don't miss him
or think about him at all;
a father has one chance
but the small parental forest
I know, I love, has many.

As I navigate the ice and snow
walking a path I've made
I hear both my father
and the voices of the trees
I have known are, for me to hear,
to take guidance from about
how I am the older man now,
and this living and aging
goes beyond the failure of a father
leaving me a happiness
in only the songs of melting ice.

NOTES ON FINDING PEACE

To stop the sound of one's footsteps
and kind of make a trade
with tall neighbourhood fir trees
and the wind winter offers the morning
seems easy when no thought is needed.
Then what is not to be called debris
can be observed all along the sidewalk
to entertain in a way both ear and eye,
caught in a crack the frost caused
in the shape of a familiar mystery,
one I figured out during other walks,
one I have found more than once,
an icy broken twig,
a tiny discarded peace sign.

NEW MUSE

To observe the gentleness,
how the peanut-half is taken
from fingers of a trusted hand,

she holds it with fierce paws
to feed today's autumnal hunger,

efficient jaws cause a chopping beat
to accompany a leaf's journey,

through periodic creaks a breeze
teaches the birch tree how to play.

MANALONE

Nothing,
if the crow is
loved by others,
is as wondrously silent
as a roost asleep
in its latest
favourite local forest.

MAKE-UP ARTIST FOR A
NEIGHBORHOOD STONE

During the invasion of a virus
throughout the smogless streets
I am thankful to use
my winter-gloved fingers
to gladly wipe away
a group of smaller stones
someone not so hopeful
chose to cover the larger stone
there on the healing earth
with a message saying,
"Don't Worry",
painted on it in yellow
and left by some brilliant child,
a hand I wish I could shake
and hold onto until forever returns.

LAST OF THE CRICKETS

Every morning I wake up
with this line
going through
my challenged mind:
"I hope this is the day
he's been shot twice
between the eyes."
Happily today a new bother
occupies my head instead
being out of the house
intentionally removed from news,
all the ongoing Trumpian dross,
I open the garden's gate
stopped by the musical legs
another inescapable line
playing over and over as the sun
lowers during a late afternoon,
as the new season called Fall
allows me to be slowly lulled
by the frightened last cricket.

INJUSTICE

As the good husband
decides to wake
and walk his son
up a street
to a good school,
he decides to stare
through what would be
another morning,
another bit of light
his eyes allow to be
what provides a new
form of thinking,
a new form of dealing
with other men,
men he must tolerate,
men he must follow
and they are not worth
following,
men at the job
he rises to go to.

After a lunch is packed,
a wife kissed goodbye,
he prepares to become
what and who he must
pretend to be,
the worker, the factory boy,
someone his employer
insists on including
in a list of other men
they have lied to,
they have mismanaged,
they have taken money from,
they have chosen
to cheat families with
for some reason.

He knows they believe
he doesn't know.

The factory is wrong,
the factory is unfortunate,
being led by dysfunction,
small men with big bellies,
led by nothing other than
small visions they see
when sitting in a bathroom,
or perhaps discussing
on a morning when they
know they will need
to lie, and look like
the honest guy
who says,
"My door is always open."

Casa Harris
April 28, 2010

HUMMINGBIRD & SHADOW

1.

If it only knew
I wouldn't make a move
the return being a third visit
to a swaying half-full feeder
early sun also adds to the floor
of the brown, chipped deck I use
to learn about how the morning
makes my head lift to help sight
be pleasantly overwhelmed, how wings
are the miracles each attempt to drink.

2.

If you only knew
I wouldn't make a move
close enough to hear faint chirps
like mysterious signals given to
make me believe there's two of you
both here for what I hope
is more than the one reason
suspended red sweetness left out
to please the thirst of you and your shadow.

HOW TO STAY ALIVE

For myself
and perhaps
for some others
it is all about
watching, no, admiring
the crystalline examples
of intelligence found
at times in the shade
on a far-too-hot afternoon,
those winged ones I share
this staying-alive thing with
flutter about
seeking the perfect branch,
no stone, or blade of grass,
to land on, knowing then
one spot, no, choice,
is to be the coolest.

HELLO!
For those self-isolating along with me
during the virus invasion, April 2020

It has been said
over and over,
"back to normal."

I stop and inquire,
"just when was that?"

GIVING SHELLS BACK TO THE SEA
In memory of Jack Sears (1929-2018)

Suddenly our home has a new room
strangely built by Death, you saying you must leave us,
but I know you have been a builder too
and, perhaps, it now is there so you can continue
to live with us, move in with us, to be felt and not seen,
build some kind of other life for us, as if the room
will always be found down a hall to the right
leading to a new spot where we'll sit with our memories,
so many and so vivid, and smile about your good life.

As I stare into one of many paintings
you made with a brush and one hand
I remember it at peace in the casket
that held you surrounded by the softest white,
what appeared to be satin, looked more like clouds,
I know it was just the body where you lived,
the one rather frail and difficult to feed, but
the one we had to hug, to now hold when we want to.
I am sure you noticed we now own your artwork
it hangs in the new room, and I take walks in
that short hallway, thankful you loved birds too.

Another place meant a great deal to your living,
in a deep part of you there was a place for the sea
you have mentioned it, but not during any talks with me,
and speaking of talks we certainly had one
that stands above the rest, still loud and word by word,
kind of a bit worrisome for me, when I sat with you
and asked for the hand of your youngest daughter –
I always hoped that meant something to you.

Today I no longer have the opportunity to ask you much
other than when I am alone and wish to say thanks not
only for her,
for how she is so much like you,
always able to be selfless, I know she carries this on,

when, really, she should be caring for herself,
a trait she asked me to help her with, and we went to
the beach named Bayfield**, one of many you treasured,
the many where you were able to find a shoreline to be a
boy once again,
choosing certain treasures brought there by the waves,
the same ones we thanked one sunny winter day, where
we too were in love,
giving the shells you chose back to the sea.

* He worked at ST. FX University for 22 years, in Antigonish, N.S.,
as well as various other positions there.

**Bayfield Beach, just out side Antigonish, N.S.

FIRST SUNDAY OF A NEW DECADE

So far among the yards
I share the season
with one sound,
small ambitious snowflakes
and the wind
hitting my furry hat,
until I turn and see
the snowman taking a bow
adding some laughter
to my walk's healing steps.

FAR FROM ANY PAYCHEQUE

I have
spent the day
observing
how the wind
removes
the night's snowfall
from the trees'
accommodating heights
in among
the wise boughs.

DOSAGE

What
morning gives
watching
the sun
turn
tiny snow-flakes
into
floating diamonds.

DARING TO LEAVE THE CAVE

Before
the Spring
is really
the new season
I feel
so alive
when
a great song
causes me
to weep,
and then
to smile.

CLING

A walk can be much more than a walk.

I did not feel like a Viking
on an unexplored shoreline.

I did not feel like a voyeur
behind a partly opened curtain.

When I was about to pass her
one chilly darkening afternoon,
when I looked up from
seeing how her child
held his half-full bottle
and noticed how the closest
tree had one leaf left.

I clearly understood we all cling
in whatever ways we must
to whatever will allow us
to come together out on any street,
out in any community no matter the size.

And such understanding came about
due to the smile of this friendly mother
with her hair and head wrapped in
a piece of material I don't need to name,

only, yes only, notice how it clings
to a choice she must've made
back where she may have been born
when she was a girl who never knew
one day on a sidewalk miles into the future
she would share a certain hello
with a thankful man born into this nation
she made another choice to come to,

a home they are able to share
under two different coloured roofs.

AWARENESS OF A CREATION

Our planet, our uproarious Earth,
where Bert protected the swallows' nests
in such a simple way, asking one day
in the granary where grandsons played
with the rings hanging from the roof,
all of us pretending to be Olympians,
being clear about no throwing stones.

All day over the pastures insects
became the food both parent birds
gathered as the cattle slept and ate
grass full of clover, or began to move
toward the gate leading back to barns,
the swallows among them for the flies
aware like all of us until he saw the end
of those selected nests we attacked, we
left behind, not old enough to remember
his request, unable to love the little bird
the years sent soaring over safe and quiet acres.

In the granary we went on playing
the day after our disregard, he found us,
told us about homes, how important
a nest becomes as eggs need to be left,
how a stone turned into a weapon we chose
to prove we were savage, we forgot,
or perhaps were about to learn by error
how much a man's hurt took over his eyes.

How he scolded the boys we were
filled with cheeping and a sight
his finger pointed to, the ruined nests
being flown to, regardless of the eggs
gone, the eggs we ended, we cried for,
how he forgave with an unforgettable hug.

AS I SIPPED A COLD BAVARIA 8.6 BEHIND THE NOVA SCOTIA COMMUNITY COLLEGE

Another September-early autumn
finds me, an easy discovery
while I rest on
the favourite of
my favoured benches,
once again knowing
the young knowledge seekers
have been returned by
the summer not quite
departed, many of them
glad, maybe grateful to
be back in the classrooms
chasing some kind of future,
unlike me, chasing nothing,
simply using my lips
in a way to believe
I am actually speaking
to the joyful chickadees,
the tiny brilliant intelligence
I listen to like I am
sitting at the front
so the teacher or prof
can hear my answer first.

AFTER LEAVING A LOUSY JOB

Another new morning
comes with
another new education:

I can finally agree
the winter is over
as spring surrounds us,

the proof once more
being how a starling
feeds one of her young
among the impatient many,

quite like the opened dandelions
and the warm mothering sun.

A VAST BLUE FRIEND

That is
what I like
about the sky:

I can stand
anywhere
and look to it
for further teachings.

A SPLITSCREEN CHRISTMAS, 2018

The sounds of a doe
we know well, eating,
her fawns in winter brown
right beside her hunger
now catching not only
the green grass still available
but filling with the night
and the neighbours' urgency
for a season I no longer trust.

All the show from yard to yard
inflatable and whirring, sadly
set up before the day of Remembrance,
more of the annual need
to be the other consumers –
not part of how the living deer
decorate their favourite lawns
to enjoy the real gifts of winter.

GAIN AND LOSS: TWO VIEWS

1.
He has a choice of shoes,
that pair he tries to step out of
each time the garden
asks him to open the gate,
asks him to become the harvestor,
the picker, the taker, the
one human voice it understands.

In the kitchen
on the counter
each crop is a colour
inside the bowl and pot he
chooses before the boil
turns into the meal.

2.
He opens a craving for rum,
after the garden is far away
the sound of the gate is echoes,
after the garden has changed him,
a man simply looking to refill
his drink, stepping off the carpet,
finding the lone fruit fly
drowned in the jigger glass
beside the spoon meant to stir
the next perfect mixture.

He dips his fingertip in
like some hero looking to save
the small body of some thing,
some tiny being none of us like.

Casa Harris
September 19, 2011

A READING OF CLOUDS*

Someone says something about a storm.

So I say what better time
to head out for a walk...
my favourite walk.

Each step allows me to see the stones again,
allows me to feel a change
one I only know as a new season.

Each look up at a vocal sky
brings what I hear,
what I question to know a sound
I dare believe is a reading of clouds...
those ones I can't name.

Those ones I see and have seen
many times when my neck needs a workout.

A reading of clouds,
each gust like a language meant for me,
why I've spent a lifetime
seeking what the sky is about
and what I will never be a part of...
left to stare and talk out loud to the wind
about whatever those clouds are named.

Each one, all of them way above
anything I might've been myself,
or the other curious men
I can say are also locked to
and led by unforgettable stories
often written about the land.

*Written between March 12-18 during the worldwide
outbreak of the Coronavirus.

A FRIEND REQUEST FOR PHILIPPE PETIT

A reason to reach out, I have many.

Among all that you shared after the towers
the one answer, " Why? There is no why!"

And me, then, saying, "How can there be no why?"
or even, "What! No why?" I guess I will learn
the answer by pressing a button
I use to share hope during this duration
caused by a virus with actual intentions,
keeping us from our dreams, from our families,
a button found among many buttons
set in some kind of order on the keyboard
now truly a daily immediate lifeline.

A need, if you will. Already hung over our lives,
connected to one side of the virus and the other
we can call beginning and ending,
a wire we kind of are all out on
holding our custom made balancing poles,
eyes on what each of us dare look at
being at so many different heights, able
to form smiles under our masked faces.

Philippe, I wonder if you will accept my request?
I promise I have no intention to ask you why
about the predictions, when the virus will end.

I just want a new friend, no matter the bridge,
no matter the cathedral, no matter the artist,
someone I, being out here using my flat feet
to understand each step will be taken, made
successfully, without doubt, willing to wait
for the others in front of me who also dare
walk the belief we can be one with the wire.

A FEATHER IN THE SUN

I no longer hear the footsteps
of a stranger from up the street
out for a morning weekend walk
with a growing little gleeful dog;
her footsteps replaced by
the continuous fury of a thirsty visitor
with wings announcing every arrival,
each one to sample a sweet blend.

How it hovers nearby, a magical buzz
insulted by the annoying saw of a neighbour
– too bad Sunday is just another day!

In between the clouds now gathering
the magic almost brought to an end
other than a particular, rapid scene:
somehow being in the right place again
the trick becomes not hearing the noise
and to follow a feather in the sun,
a feather out on the first cool breeze
brought about by a tiny preening beak.

A BRIEF MERCIFUL HUMIDITY

Time well spent
is watching
drops of cold water
disappear,
being soaked up
by a red t-shirt
promoting a woman
known as
Mary Wollstencraft Shelley.

A BRANCH OVER THE PATH

A certain morning has her
tending not only spring beds
but the path going through
a property I use to find a way
back to an old belief in short-cuts,
a path I found based on directions
another man shared, another man
thought was an easier way home.

Her name is Ruth,
unmistakably kind,
path owner of sorts, ready
to leave the bulbs and soil
in order to try and have me stop,
stop using the easy way to the job.

I listen to her reasons, her voice
nothing more than the cold morning,
her voice never saying my choice
to cut through the property she
wants to take away from humans
is a wrong choice, a choice I
think resembles the deer's,
how the does were the first to
invade the forest, Ruth said,
is a piece of her family's privacy.

No signs hang from the branch,
and what would it matter, I have
become a deer, and "Keep Out"
wouldn't have caught my eye.

Casa Harris
Nov. 21, 2011

Chad Norman, Truro, NS, Canada

His poems have appeared for nearly 40 years in literary publications across Canada, as well as a number of other countries around the world, also translated into Albanian, Spanish, Polish, Chinese, Turkish, Italian, Czech, Vietna-mese, and Hungarian.

In October 2016 he was invited by the Nordic Assn. for Canadian Studies to give talks on Canadian Poetry and read from his books at Borupgaard Gym in Copenhagen, and Risskov Gym in Aarhus, as well as other readings in both cities, and Malmo, Sweden. Because of that tour Norman has started the manuscript, *Counting Coins In Denmark And Sweden*.

In October of 2017 he read at various Eastern Canada venues in Kingston, Ottawa, and Montreal, reading poems from his Selected and New collection, published by Mosaic Press (Oakville, ON).

In October of 2018 he read at various types of venues from universities to cafes to pubs throughout Ireland, Scotland, Wales, while there he visited Swansea and slept three nights in the room where Dylan Thomas was born. A celebration of Canadian Poetry took place during this tour too.

His most recent books are Simona: A Celebration Of The S.P.C.A., out 2021 from Cyberwit. Net Press (India), Squall: Poems In The Voice of Mary Shelley, 2020, Guernica Editions (Toronto), A Matter Of Inclusion, 2022, Mwanaka Media And Publishing (Zimbabwe), and a children's picture book, B And Boy, 2023, Cyberwit. Net (India).

He is currently a member of The League Of Canadian Poets.

www.ingramcontent.com/pod-product-compliance
Lightning Source LLC
Chambersburg PA
CBHW071114120626
46546CB00003B/1336